Social Loafing
The Career Choice of Workplace Slackers

Louis Bevoc

Published by
NutriNiche System LLC

Louis Bevoc books...simple explanations of complex subjects

Introduction	4
Related theories and effects	6
Organizational occurrences	9
Cultural influence	10
Sucker influence	11
Free-rider influence	12
Lack of significance	13
Lack of unity	15
Lack of skills	16
Lack of ambition	17
Lack of urgency	18
Lack of monitoring	19
Lack of compensation	20
Lack of contribution	21
Consequences	22
Decreased motivation	23
Increased absenteeism	25
Decreased teamwork	26
Contagiousness	34
Career choice	37
Education and training	38
Job skills	38
Upbringing	42
Interests	42

    Age   43
    Culture and religion   43

Prevention   45
    Establish goals   45
    Monitor team sizes   47
    Establish individual responsibilities   48
    Establish written procedures   48
    Monitor team member selection   49
    Provide feedback on team progress   49
    Require team members to rate each other   50
    Promote a teamwork culture   50

Summary   50

Introduction

What is social loafing? Max Ringelmann, an agricultural engineer and inventor from France, first introduced the phenomenon in 1913. He said social loafing occurs in groups. Specifically, in regards to accomplishing tasks and objectives, people give less effort when working in groups then they give working alone.

Mr. Ringelmann based his thinking on the now academically famous *rope-pulling studies.* This research had people pull on a rope as hard as they could pull and the pressure they exerted was measured and recorded. He then repeated the pulling with two people or more people and found that as the number of people increased the amount of effort per person decreased. The total amount of pressure increased as the group size increased, but the pressure applied by each person went down. These findings became known as the Ringelmann effect and were the start of research that was termed social loafing by psychologists.

Many years later, in the mid-1970s, Ringelmann's research was replicated with a few changes. Two groups were used in this study. The first group was the same makeup as that used in Ringelmann's work and the results duplicated his findings. The second group, however, was staged with mostly actors pretending to be randomly selected participants along with a few real participants. The actors gave very little effort and faked pulling the rope. Interestingly, the real participants were less likely to slack in the second group where nobody else was exerting effort; thereby indicating that social loafing is less of a concern when several group members refuse to contribute. This indication needs more research to determine if it has any validity, but the first group in the replication study supports Ringelmann's thinking about social loafing.

In the late 1970s, a study conducted by Latané, Williams, & Harkins was published in the *Journal of Personality and Social Psychology* that made the concept of social loafing much more well-known in academic circles. This study had the participants yell or clap as loudly as possible by themselves and in groups. Findings showed that the noise made by the participants was louder when they were alone than it was when they were in a group. In other words, the group setting caused the individual members to engage in social loafing.

Latané, Williams, & Harkins were intrigued by the results and decided to take their research further in the hopes of gaining more knowledge about the subject matter. Their next study explored the psychological influence of social loafing on people's behavior. They wanted to see if merely thinking about being part of a group was enough to cause people to engage in social loafing. Their research involved blindfolding the participants and having them wear headphones to block out all vision and hearing. They were then told that they were in a group with other participants who were yelling with them. In reality, there was no group and they were yelling by themselves. The results found that people who thought they were in a group were not as loud as when they were alone; thereby supporting the idea that social loafing occurs in groups even if the group is only thought to exist.

Fast forward to 2005, and another significant study was done on social loafing. This research focused on group size and its impact on the performance of group members. Half of the groups used in the study consisted of eight members while the other half consisted of four members. Some of the groups were moved to a table where they worked together on solving a problem while other groups separated the members and had them work individually on computers, communicating only electronically while solving a problem together. In all cases, findings showed that members exhibited greater effort when placed in smaller groups; thereby indicating that larger groups allow for more social loafing.

Related theories and effects

It should be noted that social loafing has been compared to another theory proposed by psychologists. This theory is known as the *diffusion of responsibility* and it explains the reasons why people give less effort. Essentially, it is built around the premise that people feel less responsible for taking action in a given situation when other people are present who could also take action.

In the late 1960s, researchers John Darley and Bibb Latané conducted a now-famous study testing the diffusion of responsibility in emergency situations. This study was done for academic reasons, but it was also designed to help law enforcement after a tragic occurrence. In 1964, a young lady named Kitty Genovese was murdered. The circumstances of this homicide captured the attention of people all over the nation. Kitty was stabbed across the street from where she lived in an apartment on Austin Street in Kew Gardens, Queens, New York City. A few weeks after the murder, it was discovered that over 35 people witnessed or heard the attack taking place, but none of these people took any action to help her. They did not call the police or come to her aid, and she was left alone to die. Darley and Latané wanted to help New York Police better understand why nobody reacted during Ms. Genovese's murder, and they thought their study might shed some light on the reasons.

The study had participants sit in different rooms. They could not see or hear each other, and their only communication was over an intercom system. Sometimes the participants thought they were in a one-on-one discussion with a planted person (confederate) leading the conversation, while other times they thought they were engaged in a group discussion with a planted person (confederate) leading the conversation. However, regardless of the number of people thought to be involved, the planted leader (confederate) always pretended to have a seizure to see if the participants would react and offer help by leaving the room and telling someone. Results showed that the participants were less likely to get help if they thought another person in the group might do so. In other words, if they thought they were in a one-on-one discussion, then they reacted quickly and went for help, but if they thought they were in a group, then they spent more time thinking about whether or not to react.

The results of the research conducted by Darley and Latanés also help explain why nobody reacted when Kitty Genovese was being killed. People that heard or saw the violent actions knew that others were also hearing or seeing the same thing so they did nothing because they assumed those others would call the appropriate authorities and seek or provide medical assistance. However, regardless of the validity of the diffusion of responsibility theory, it is not necessarily the only reason why people did not react. For example, some people might not have been comfortable playing any type of leadership role in a situation so they sat back and waited for someone else to make a move. Other people might not have been sure if the situation truly was an emergency, especially since nobody else was reacting, and they did not want to embarrass themselves if they assumed it was an emergency and turned out to be wrong. Last, but certainly not least, some people might simply have been unsure about what action they should have taken. Should they have called the police, got a neighbor who might know about these types of situations, or went to the crime scene and offered personal assistance? Since they were unsure of what to do, they did nothing. Today, they could use their cell phone to immediately call 911 and let the operators decide what action to take, but 911 was not available in 1964 and cell phones were non-existent. Anyway, based on the circumstances people find themselves in, it is understandable why some do not take action in emergency situations.

Let's take this discussion a little deeper to see how the diffusion of responsibility theory works in a long-term real-world crisis situation. Does this theory explain the reason that people did not help Jewish people during Nazi Germany's reign of terror during World War II? Maybe to a limited extent, but there were also other factors involved that were probably more responsible. People felt a diminished responsibility to help the Jews because they thought others could do so, but they also feared for their lives and the lives of their families. Individuals caught helping Jews were subject to being killed by the Nazis on the spot, with no trial, along with some of their family members who were selected as part of the punishment.

The holocaust shows how the diffusion of responsibility theory is not always applicable when trying to understand the reasoning for people's lack of action during crisis situations. However, it does have some usefulness in determining why some individuals feel less responsible for providing help in situations where others are present who could also take action. Social loafing is a reality that has been around as long as groups of people have existed, and it is likely not going away anytime in the future.

Now you understand some of the research that has helped developed social loafing as a phenomenon and an interesting area of study. Armed with this knowledge, let's move forward to a discussion on social loafing in the workplace...the reason behind the writing of this book.

Organizational occurrences

Social loafing is an interesting topic that expands beyond the walls of academic research. In addition to being an interesting area of study for college professors, it is a phenomenon that impacts most people at some time in their lives. They might not even realize it is happening, but it does take place and the effects can be quite substantial. For example, many students have experienced social loafing in educational settings...specifically undergraduate college courses. There often seems to be those one or two group members who want to do the minimum to get by, and this tends to annoy other affiliates since they have to carry extra weight. This is an age-old problem that has gone on since groups were formed.

Social loafing also occurs in organizations. However, it differs from education because it is more permanent. Students typically work together for a semester, and their groups disband when the course ends. Workplace teams often last longer...often times until a project is completed. Worse yet, hardworking employees sometimes have to work with social loafers for many years after teams have disbanded. This is a constant reminder of the extra work they had to perform due to the social loafers' refusal to contribute their fair share.

Based on the above, it's rather easy to see that social loafing can produce some negative effects. However, before we get into these effects, we need to discuss the reasons why this phenomenon occurs. The following are some common causes of social loafing using organizational examples for support and clarification:

Cultural influence

Culture is the most influential aspect of some people's lives. Certain cultures encourage social loafing while others discourage it. The United States, for example, tends to promote social loafing in workplaces because the major focus is on individual accomplishments. Group accomplishments reflect the group as a whole, not the individual, and this holds less importance for many employees. Americans prefer the accolades that come with individual achievements, so they give more effort when working alone then they do when working in groups.

Asians, on the other hand, view group accomplishments differently. They are less likely to social loaf due to the value their culture places on group accomplishments. Asians feel the accomplishments of the team reflect on them personally, so they tend to work harder when collaborating with others.

> *Organizational example*
>
> Zachary is a vice president at the United States division of an international automotive supplier. He is working on a team project with four other vice presidents from divisions in Japan, China, South Korea, and the Philippines. The team's goal is to find faster ways to get products to market using existing channels of distribution.
>
> The team assembles and starts to assign tasks. The Japanese, Filipino, Chinese and South Korean vice

presidents all welcome the opportunity for involvement. Zachary gladly lets them take responsibility because his interest in this team project takes a back seat to a marketing plan that he is currently working on by himself. If he succeeds with the marketing plan, he will establish the respect and credibility necessary to make him a legitimate candidate for the US president's job when it becomes available next year. Success on the team project will credit the group as a whole, and it will not showcase Zachary's individual talents.

In short, the business culture of the United States promotes Zachary's behavior. He is more likely to be promoted based on his individual achievements, and this leads to his social loafing on the team.

Sucker influence

In general, people do not want to feel like they are being taken advantage of by others. In group settings, they avoid volunteering due to fear that others will stick them with the majority of the work. An example is a booster club for a boy's high school football team. Parents of the players are strongly encouraged to help out with booster club activities. However, very few parents volunteer because they do not want to end up doing the majority of the work. They believe that once they start taking on responsibilities, the coaches will assume that they can handle other tasks and ask them to do more.

Organizational example

Clara works as a salesperson at a window installation company. The company plans to have a holiday party for all employees and their families, and volunteers are needed to help organize the event. As a recruitment method, management sends out an email to all employees asking for their assistance. Clara wants to volunteer to set up the decorations, but she does not want this to lead to other duties being assigned to her. She is afraid that she will end up being responsible for food, entertainment, and clean-up for the party.

Ultimately, Clara decides to hold off on volunteering in order to avoid becoming a sucker. She becomes a social loafer so other employees are not able to take advantage of her.

Free-rider influence

Some individuals are aware that they will receive credit for the group performance regardless of their efforts, so they choose to take a free-ride at the expense of others. An example of this involves a protest march. Everyone in the group marches to the point of destination, but some people choose not to speak up once they arrive. They simply sit back and watch while others voice their opinions about the cause. The non-vocal protesters receive credit for being part of the protest group, but they are not involved in some of the most important work because their efforts are not necessary.

Organizational example

Sara works at the headquarters of a retail clothing store chain. She is upset because management has decided that the company will no longer offer dental insurance to employees. She joins a group of 20 other employees who schedule a meeting with the president to discuss the loss of their dental program.

The group meets with the president in a conference room, but only four members speak up during the meeting (Sara is not one of them). They voice their displeasure with the change and, as a result, the president decides to extend dental coverage for another 60 days while management revisits the cost issue to see if the program can be continued.

This is a victory for the protesting group of employees, and Sara receives credit for being part of that group. However, she receives this credit without saying a word during the meeting.

Ultimately, four employees in the group did the majority of the work while the rest of the members were social loafers who benefitted as free riders.

Lack of significance

People become social loafers when they do not believe that their contributions matter. It's not that they don't care; it's that they don't believe effort on their part will make a difference.

One example of insignificance involves voting for people who have been nominated for the board of director positions at a large mutual fund. Small investors believe their votes will not make a difference, so they throw their ballots in the trash when they receive them. If those same investors were part of a 10-person committee that determined the board members' status, they likely would have taken their voting rights much more seriously.

Another example of insignificance involves boycotting. A woman might not like the fact that a world-wide tuna fish producer kills dolphins while fishing for tuna. However, the tuna company is so large that the woman believes her boycott of their tuna will not make any difference, so she continues to buy their products. If this woman bought her tuna directly from a local fisherman who killed dolphins while fishing, she would have been more likely to boycott his business.

Organizational example

Hargrove Manufacturing employs over 1200 people. The company is considering implementing a profit-sharing plan, and management has been asking for input from employees regarding their level of interest. So far, the comments have been overwhelmingly in favor of the plan. Over 450 employees have responded, and 95% like the idea.

Marcus is a production worker at the Hargrove, and he wants the profit-sharing plan to be implemented. However, after hearing about the large number of employees that have indicated they support the idea, he decides not to submit his own comments.

In short, Marcus is a social loafer because he does not believe his contributions will matter. He cares about the profit-sharing plan and wants it implemented, but he does not believe effort on his part is significant enough to make a difference in the outcome.

Lack of unity

Teams lack unity when members fail to bond and establish good working relationships. Lack of unity causes social loafing because members are not concerned with helping each other achieve the objectives of the team. An example is a church choir where the members do not get along with each other. Every time they hold a practice, at least two members do not show up. This is detrimental to the choir since their goal is to get better…and that will not happen if all members are not present. In short, the members who skip practice are not concerned about the choir due to the lack of unity within.

Organizational example

Renee works in quality control for a computer printer manufacturer. She has been assigned to a team with a production employee, a research & development employee, and an accounting employee. The goal of the team is to find areas where costs can be reduced in production.

The team has met twice a week for the past three weeks, but Renee has not established a comfort level at the meetings. She has not been able to bond with the other members, and this is causing her to lose interest in the cost savings objective of the team. She starts to focus on other job-related tasks that she finds more interesting, and the team moves to the back burner in terms of importance.

Renee is a social loafer because she has not been able to establish a good working relationship with the other members. This lack of unity causes her to lose interest in helping others achieve the goals of the team.

Lack of skills

When people work with others who lack skills, they are inclined to reduce their own performance and become social loafers. An example is a student who volunteers to work on the technical crew for the high school musical. He is very tech-savvy and wants to add a variety of technical effects to the performance. However, after meeting the rest of the technical crew, he realizes that none of them have achieved his level of skill and expertise, so he tones down his idea and makes the musical much simpler in terms of technology.

Organizational example

Shannon is starting a new position as a laboratory supervisor. She has a very good understanding of laboratory procedures, and she plans to completely revamp the microbiological program by adding modern methodology and making it government certified. However, after she starts her job, she realizes the existing lab technicians are not capable of taking the lab to the next level. She could hire more skilled personnel who understand her needs, but instead, she decides to make things easier on everyone by foregoing her idea of upgrading and certifying the microbiology program.

Shannon is a social loafer because she decided not to upgrade and certify the microbiology laboratory. She realized the skill level of her technicians was not equal to her own, so she chose to simplify matters and take an easier route.

Lack of ambition

Sometimes people's lack of ambition causes them to become social loafers. Their goal is to work as little as possible, and they plan accordingly to achieve that goal. An example is a football who fakes an injury during practice so he does not have to run for conditioning. He likes playing football, but he has no desire to run.

Organizational example

Stanley is a stock person at a hardware store. He does not really care about his job, has no desire to grow with the company, and does not plant to become a long-term employee. He remains employed at the hardware store because he needs money and has no desire to look elsewhere for a job.

Today a customer needs Stanley's assistance. She cannot find roofing nails, and she asks Stanley if the store has any in stock. Without bothering to look, Stanley tells her that everything they have is on the store shelf. In reality, there are five cases of roofing nails in the stockroom, but Stanley has no desire to retrieve them for the customer.

Stanley is a social loafer due to his lack of ambition. He does whatever is necessary to avoid work...even if it means lying to customers.

Lack of urgency

People who believe others are handling everything tend to relax and not contribute their fair share. They don't react until the situation becomes desperate or urgent...and this typically does not occur when other people are willing to do the work. An example is an adult male who still lives with his parents. His mother has cooked his meals and done his laundry for his entire life, so he is able to sit back and essentially do nothing. He will only need to contribute if his mother decides to stop doing the work for him...and this is likely not going to happen.

Organizational example

Melanie is a customer service representative at a windshield replacement company. A light bulb has burned out on her desk lamp. She knows a new bulb is located less than 100 feet away from her desk, but Instead of replacing it, she calls for maintenance.

Melanie is a social loafer because she knows the maintenance department will handle her problem. She will not replace the bulb herself if other people are available to do the work for her. If nobody is available and limited light prevents her from doing her work, then she will change the bulb.

Lack of monitoring

Many people need structure in order to be productive. Part of that structure involves monitoring of the activities they are performing...and that monitoring often comes in the form of supervision.

Lack of monitoring can create problems. An example includes a man who is running for a position in congress. He stops in Baltimore, Maryland to make a campaign speech. However, none of the people on his Baltimore team were instructed on how to prepare for his speech, so nothing is ready when he arrives. The entire staff social loafed because their preparation activities were not monitored.

Organizational example

Aaron works for a mortgage broker that strongly believes in teamwork when dealing with customers. He works with six other employees on a sales team, and their job is to contact potential customers for business.

The team reports to Helen, but she is out of the office most of the day. She checks back at the end of the day to review sales, but she is not actively involved in supervising her employees.

Aaron takes advantage of Helen's absence. He does personal work at his computer, takes extended lunches, and talks with other employees when he is supposed to be working. Due to Helen's lack of monitoring, Aaron is a social loafer.

Lack of compensation

Some people become social loafers when they believe they are not being equally compensated for their efforts. An example is a middle school student who receives worse grades than other students in her classroom. Her grades are upsetting to her, so she starts to withdraw and no longer participates in group discussions. Her perception of the situation and resulting attitude turn her into a social loafer.

Organizational example

Ann works with three other women in the office of a home insulation company. These ladies do general office work that includes answering phones and taking orders, and they report to the owner of the company Elisha.

Throughout the year, Elisha gives the office women rewards for doing a good job. Examples include gift certificates for massages or dinner, baseball or theater tickets, or $50 cash to spend on whatever they desire.

Ann has not received a reward from Elisha for the past nine months. All three other women have received awards during this time period, and this is upsetting to Ann. She feels like her efforts are being overlooked, and this causes her to do less work. She waits until one of the other ladies answers phone calls, and she does not volunteer to take on extra tasks during busy periods. In short, Ann's perceived lack of compensation causes her to become a social loafer.

Lack of contribution

It is fairly common for people to become social loafers when they believe that they are doing more work than others. They view other people doing less work, and this causes them to lower their efforts as a form of retaliation. An example involves two boys, George and Andy, doing landscape work at their father's house. Andy stops work on two separate occasions to talk to his girlfriend on his cell phone. This upsets George because he continually works while Andy does little to contribute. During Andy's third phone call, George stops working and lies down on a hammock in an attempt to equalize the workload.

Organizational example

Gary is a commercial plumber. He is currently working on a big job with another plumber named Stephen. Over a two-week period, Stephen has left the work site more than five times to "check on a job" at a different location. Each time Stephen leaves, he is gone for more than two hours…and this is very upsetting to Gary because he is left alone to do the work.

One day, after Stephen returns from his "job check," Gary tells him that he has to work at a different location. He goes home and does not return for the rest of the day. This is Gary's way of retaliating for all the time that Stephen has missed.

In short, Gary became a social loafer due to Stephen's lack of contribution. The most interesting thing about this situation is that social loafing caused a person to become a social loafer.

Now you are aware of some common reasons why people choose to engage in social loafing. Next, let's move into a discussion on the consequences of this phenomenon.

Consequences

There are many problems associated with social loafing. Some are rather obvious while some are not so obvious depending on the visibility of the issue. For example, an obvious consequence of social loafing is a team's loss of productivity. Teams are assembled with designated members who all possess different skills. When one or more people do not contribute, the combination of skill is lost and productivity suffers.

An example of a less obvious consequence is absenteeism. People might get fed up and decide to miss work due to a social loafer, but it is hard to tell if social loafing is the cause since so many other factors impact the reason why people miss work. However, it can be said with confidence that everything listed below is a consequence of social loafing.

Decreased motivation

When people witness social loafing going on within the groups that they are a part of, they become demotivated. Instead of wanting to perform at peak levels, they do the minimum to get by. This is based on the unequal distribution of workload that they are experiencing. In other words, they perceive actions by social loafers as unfair to the other group members since those other group members are forced to burden more of the responsibility for accomplishing goals and objectives.

Decreased motivation due to perceived social loafing is best explained by the *equity theory*. Behavioral psychologist J. Stacy Adams originated the idea that employees compare their work-related contributions and results (inputs) to the same of other employees and make determinations based on what they perceive. In this regard, they are searching for equity between themselves and others in the form of recognition and rewards (outcomes).

The basic thinking behind the equity theory is that employees value fair and equitable treatment because it motivates them to perform their jobs to the best of their abilities. Employees who feel under-rewarded or under-compensated become upset, and they strive to create situations that they feel are fair to everyone. Employees who feel over-rewarded or over-compensated also strive for change. The guilt they experience leads them to make an attempt at creating equality in their situations.

The Equity Theory is very useful for measuring job satisfaction. If employees believe their coworkers are being recognized or rewarded more for less contributions, then they become dissatisfied with their jobs. This theory promotes the thinking that, in order to attain job satisfaction, rewards and recognition (outcomes) must be directly and consistently related to employee contributions (inputs). Social loafers do not contribute, so they should not be recognized for their efforts. In fact, their lack of effort should be pointed out and they should be excluded from any type of reward. Unfortunately, this calling out typically does not happen because groups are often rewarded as a whole and every member is recognized regardless of their input or lack of input.

An example of social loafing that causes decreased motivation is Ralph, an assembler at a bicycle shop. Ralph believes he works very hard and thinks he is doing much more work than the other two assemblers. This perceived unfairness upsets Ralph because all three employees make the same hourly wage.

Ralph is so bitter that he decides to scale back his work production. He purposely slows down to a pace that he thinks is equal to the other two assemblers. The owner of the shop notices the lack of production, but does not take any action because he cannot afford to give raises, and he needs all three of the assemblers in order to meet his customer demands.

In this particular case, Ralph's response to the perceived "inequity" is a decrease in personal workload and a negative attitude. This response is his attempt to eliminate the inequity, although it does little to resolve the actual problem.

Increased absenteeism

Absenteeism in workplaces can be attributed to many different workplace factors, and it is difficult to determine which factor is the most important. However, social loafing is one of these factors because, quite simply, people get upset when others social loaf and show their anger by missing work.

Absenteeism is employees' unscheduled absence from their jobs. The keyword here is "unscheduled." Scheduled absences can be planned for in advance, and this helps avoid some of the potential problems that might occur during the employees' time off. However, there is very little time to plan for unscheduled absences, and the necessary resources might not be available on a moment's notice.

Leaders in organizations are not naive enough to think employees are going to be at work on every scheduled day. They expect workers to miss some time because they are not feeling well or want to attend to personal matters that conflict with the times they are supposed to be at work. This is acceptable and does not present a problem…unless it becomes excessive.

When absenteeism becomes excessive, it is a major headache for organizations. If employees do not show up for work, then their jobs need to be performed by someone else. If no one else is available, then those jobs simply do not get done. This creates difficult and stressful situations for workers and managers, and it occurs far too often in some workplaces.

Absenteeism has a greater impact on smaller organizations than it does on larger ones due to the size of the workforces. For example, a business with 100 employees will function close to normal if five people are absent. However, a business with eight employees might operate if five workers are missing.

Regardless of the number of employees in the workplace, excessive absenteeism causes problems. It stresses out the employees who are forced to take on additional workloads, lowers morale, and affects productivity. Ultimately, it impacts the financial well-being of organizations as they struggle to meet the needs of their customers.

Since there are problems associated with absenteeism, leaders of organizations need to do whatever they can to minimize it. This starts by gaining a better understanding of the causes and those causes include social loafing.

Decreased teamwork

Teams are major building blocks of organizations. They have replaced individuals in an attempt to satisfy complex customer demands and resolve internal issues. They utilize personnel that help solve problems faster and more accurately. Employees are selected for teams based on their position, skill, knowledge, and capacity to lead others. The assembled group is well equipped to find solutions to problems based on their experience, understanding, and capability.

Social loafing can damage relationships between members of teams. This damage is similar to that experienced when social loafers impact normal coworker relationships, but it is actually more severe because team members are forced to communicate fairly intensely for periods of time that can be lengthy. If they do not like each other, then they risk failing to accomplish goals and objectives.

It is important that team members work together effectively and efficiently because they provide many advantages for organizations. These advantages include the following:

Synergy

This might be the biggest advantage of teams because every member can exchange thoughts and entertain other perspectives. Each employee has unique strengths that add diversity to the team, and the differing viewpoints contribute to the overall effectiveness. The synergy involved improves decision-making and helps the team reach goals within limited time frames.

Organizational example

Dontrell is a salesperson employed by a pen and pencil manufacturer. He wants to create a pen that will write upside down due to a growing market trend that he has identified. When he approaches the CEO about his idea, she thinks it is good and tells him she is going to set up a team that must bring the pen to production in three months.

The CEO sets up a diverse team of six employees. She selects the members based on their skills and knowledge, and the reasons behind her choices are as follows:

Dontrell is on the team because he has the drive and vision necessary to complete the project. He also understands the market and knows what the pen needs to look like in order to sell. For instance, he knows the thickness, length, style, and ink color needed. Dontrell is the leader of the team. His role is critical for generating initial discussion and coordinating activities between members.

Sandy is placed on the team because of her designer skills. She can create just about anything on her computer, and this will give the group several options. She can draw a pen with a cap, she can make it retractable, or she can add a pocket clip. With the click of a button, she can change the outer shell or ink color. The best part of Sandy's ability is the fact that she knows how to use a 3D printer, so she can create actual prototypes for the group to evaluate. Sandy is the creative and technical person on the team. Her role is critical for the visual presentation of the finished product.

Jacqueline is part of the team because she understands manufacturing. She knows what it takes to produce the product. She can answer questions about labor costs, machinery required, and time needed. Jacqueline's role is necessary for bringing the pen from concept to finished product.

Bart's quality skills make him a team member. He understands the problems that can result during manufacturing and implements quality tests and procedures to prevent them. He compares the color of the outer shell, measures ink flow, and tests the durability of the pen. Bart's role is necessary to make sure the finished product functions as specified.

Lisa's ability to obtain resources places her on the team. She is an experienced buyer of supplies for the manufacturing plant and understands pricing and availability. She will let the members know if they are making decisions that are not feasible in terms or purchasing. Lisa's role prevents the team from wasting time on ideas that are too costly or too impractical.

Andrew is part of the team for information gathering purposes. He is an attorney who is an experienced researcher. He needs to make sure that the pen they create is not patented by another person or organization. Andrew's role is to protect the group from future litigation.

Efficiency

Teams are able to move faster and more effectively than individuals acting alone. This is because they make the most of member's individual strengths and talents. In areas where some people are weak, others are strong...and their combined efforts work together to solve problems.

The best part about the efficiency of a team is that it gets better as the team bonds. Over time, members learn the strengths of others in the group and utilize those strengths when they are needed.

>Organizational example
>
>Miranda is part of a team working to resolve a flooring issue at a warehouse. Traffic from forklifts and floor jacks is damaging the floor, and it is reaching a point where it will soon be dangerous for workers.
>
>Miranda has a good understanding of warehouse operations. She knows what equipment is needed to get the job done, and she understands the roles of every employee since she has worked all of their jobs during her 15-year career.
>
>Miranda, however, is not familiar with the types of flooring material needed to resolve the problem. She's not sure if epoxy, cement, or another type of polymer is the best solution. She needs help because she wants to find a permanent solution in order to avoid a reoccurrence of the same problem in the future.
>
>Richard is another team member that provides Miranda with the help she needs. He has experienced similar flooring problems and recommends eight-inch thick cement because he knows epoxy materials cannot

withstand the heavy traffic issues. Richard's suggestion leads to a decision being made, and the floor is repaired before it poses danger to any employees.

Richard was strong in an area where Miranda needed help. They efficiently worked together to find a solution to a problem and prevent a potential safety hazard.

Flexibility

Different personalities on a team help the team accept change. Some people find change challenging or stressful, while others embrace it. This is because people react differently to the same situations based on their perceptions, and those perceptions give teams the flexibility needed to accept change.

Organizational example

Veronica and Matthew are on a team that has been assembled to find a better method of evaluating employee performance. One suggestion is to get employees involved in their own evaluation by providing feedback to their boss during their review.

Veronica is afraid to change the current system because she fears some employees will not like this new procedure. Mathew has a different perspective on the proposed method. He worked for another company that used the employee feedback appraisal system, and employees were very happy with it.

Mathew informs Veronica and the rest of the team about his experience, and this reassures them that the employees will like the new method. The team accepts the change and recommends the implementation of the new evaluation system.

Idea generation

People have different experiences that add to the way they think about situations. Team member's individual thoughts generate unique ideas that can be bounced off the rest of the group for problem-solving. This process generates the best ideas because they are evaluated by everyone before being implemented as solutions.

Organizational example

Rafael works for an international company called Jalen Industries. He worked for the Brazilian division of the company for seven years before transferring to the headquarters in the United States, and he has now been assigned to a team responsible for improving employee morale and commitment.

Team members suggest a company picnic, a volleyball tournament, a bowling league, and a free massage therapist as potential solutions. These are all good ideas, but Rafael experienced something unique in Brazil that those employees found very beneficial. Many different species of exotic animals are owned by people in South America, so the Brazilian division hired a full-time veterinarian that treated any employee's pet free of charge. This worked wonders for employee morale, and a survey showed that it was the major reason that employees were committed to Jalen Industries.

Rafael suggests that Jalen incorporate a similar dental program in the United States. Any employee or immediate family member is eligible to receive free dental treatment from a full-time dentist hired by the company. Other team members discuss this idea, and cannot find any negatives, so they implement the plan. Rafael's thoughts led to this unique idea based on the experience he had in Brazil.

Divided responsibilities

Teams divide responsibilities between group members, and this prevents individual employees from being overloaded with work. It also allows members to support each other through cooperation and mutual understanding. In short, dividing responsibilities alleviates the stress associated with being completely responsible for a project.

Organizational example

Cassandra is an IT person who is part of a team that is charged with purchasing new office software for a staff of 90 employees. The team wants to research six different types of programs, and Cassandra's expertise is essential for making a decision. However, Cassandra does not have time to do everything involved with the research because she has tasks outside of the team that need to be completed.

The team decides that Cassandra will make the final decision on the program to purchase, but they will set everything up for her. Rhonda is put in charge of contacting vendors for program demonstrations, John negotiates pricing to get the best possible deals, Erika looks at the ergonomic benefits, and Tony conducts a survey to see if there are specific employee needs that need to be incorporated. Cassandra's role is to evaluate the programs for their overall capabilities and make a selection based on her findings.

Team members realized that one person would have difficultly handling every aspect of this project, so they divided the responsibilities in order to prevent Cassandra from becoming stressed due to work overload.

As you now know, teams are very beneficial to organizations and the employees working in them. However, like many other aspects of business, they are not a catch-all solution for every concern….and that will be discussed in the next section.

Based on the above, it is rather easy to see why a consequence of social loafing can be decreased teamwork. Without that teamwork employees and organizations suffer because goals and objectives are not achieved.

Contagiousness

This consequence might actually be the worst on the list. Quite simply, if not controlled, social loafing can spread from one person to another because employees typically spend a lot of time interacting with each other. In fact, barring those who travel extensively or work remotely, some employees spend more time with their coworkers than they do with their family and friends. When coworkers spend this much time together, disagreements are unavoidable and some of those disagreements revolve around the amount of work being done. Employees get in arguments about who does the most work and, if these arguments are not resolved, relationships start to dissolve and conflict becomes the norm. At this point, employees who normally do their fair share of work tend to give up and join the crowd of social loafers. They do not want the grief that goes along with properly doing their jobs, so they take what appears to be the easiest way to work and get along with others.

Social loafing might be the easiest method for conformation with others, but it does nothing for the health of the organizations. Growth and prosperity give way to apathy and neglect, and everyone ends up suffering due to the cancer that spreads through the workforce. This negative behavior also reduces a sense of belonging for all workers as they experience unhappiness and job dissatisfaction.

Unfortunately, the effects of negative behavior are greater than that of positive behavior. As more and more employees become social loafers, motivation and performance decrease and people stop sharing information and ideas. Teams experience increased conflict and employees spend more time avoiding each other than they do working toward the resolution of problems. Over time, these effects can become so severe that they lead to the demise of organizations.

It should also be noted that a consequence of contagiousness known as groupthink has the potential to rear its ugly head. Psychologist Irving Janis established the term "groupthink" to describe a process in which a group can make irrational decisions. In groupthink situations involving social loafing, group members do not want to put in the effort to help make decisions so they attempt to conform to what they believe to be the consensus of the group. The end result is the group ultimately agreeing on something that each member might view as unwise if they had the motivation to contribute their own thoughts and ideas.

As might be expected, groupthink defeats the entire purpose of group decision making because ideas are stymied and synergy is virtually non-existent. Decisions are made that are not well thought or analyzed; thereby resulting in employees and organizations suffering the consequences.

Organizational example

A team of employees at the headquarters of a restaurant chain is asked to evaluate race relations in the organization. Several members have no interest in what is being discussed so they do not express their opinions. Instead, these members indicate that there are no major issues because they believe that is what everyone wants to hear.

The group agreed that there were no race problems in the restaurant chain even though they thought differently. They conformed to what they believed was the consensus of the group, and this destroyed the group synergy. It also did nothing to achieve the organizational objective of evaluating race relations.

Contagiousness is a consequence of social loafing that can negatively impact an entire organization. It creates an apathetic environment that makes it difficult for anyone to get motivated or make the changes necessary to accomplish goals and objectives. Based on its destructive potential, leaders need to understand the importance of controlling social loafing to prevent it from becoming a workplace norm.

Career choice

This book is based on the thinking that social loafing is a career choice for workplace slackers. In order to expand on that thinking, it is necessary to understand what is involved with making a career choice. Let's move into a discussion on the factors involved in making career choices and the relationships of those factors to social loafers.

Not surprisingly, many different factors influence people's career choices. They want to know the basics about the job they are interested in such as prerequisite requirements, responsibilities, and compensation, but other factors also play a role...some of which are quite visible and others that are hidden beneath the surface. These factors are listed below along with a description and their relationship with social loafers.

Education and training

Some careers require a lot of classroom work and training before people working within them can become officially licensed, certified, or qualified. For example, obtaining a license to practice psychiatry can take eight years of classroom work along with several years of residency. People who do not want to spend a lot of time going to school or training for a job should probably not select a medical doctor as a career choice.

Interestingly, some people have undergone extensive education and training and still choose to be social loafers at their places of employment. This choice shows that social loafing is not limited by job type or compensation.

Job Skills

Every job requires skills in order to effectively and efficiently perform the tasks involved. Some of these skills are simple while others are not so simple, but, regardless of the complexity, they are needed for peak job performance. In short, people lacking specific skills are not able to move into careers that require them.

It would be virtually impossible to list every job skill for every career. However, these skills can be classified into three basic types. These three types are hard skills, soft skills, and transferable skills, and they are described below for a better understanding of what they are, how they are obtained, what types of careers they are used in, and their relationship with social loafers.

Hard skills

Also known as technical skills, hard skills are typically learned and can be measured and evaluated. People's proficiency with these skills is usually based on the time and effort they put into learning them. They often undergo this learning in classrooms, but it is also conducted via webinars, seminars, videos, podcasts, and on the job training. Hard skills can also be learned in non-traditional ways such as role-playing, acting, games, and competitions. However, regardless of the method, hard skills are usually learned and they are important when choosing a career.

Examples of hard skills include reading, writing, math, science, accounting, and economics. People with strong math and science skills might be good engineers while those with excellent reading and writing skills might be good editors. Obviously, there is no guarantee that people will succeed in a chosen career simply because they have the required hard skills, but they stand a much better chance than those who do not possess those skills.

It is not uncommon for social loafers to possess hard skills. They might have undergone training to acquire those skills (possibly while exhibiting social loafing behavior during the training), but they choose not to use them in their careers. They do as little work as possible, make sure they have lighter workloads than their coworkers, and take credit for accomplishments that others have made without their contributions.

Soft skills

In recent years, soft skills have gained mainstream popularity and grown in importance for leaders of organizations. This is due to the realization that soft skills are important in workplaces and they are often lacking by employees with strong hard skills.

Soft skills are skills used to get along with others during interpersonal relationships. They include listening, empathy, communication, etiquette, manners, and understanding. These skills can be learned through education and training, but they typically develop over time as employees mature and gain experience. Workers learn through trial and error what they need to do to form relationships with their coworkers. These relationships can then be used for information sharing, advice gathering, and decision-making help that makes everyone's job easier.

People in leadership positions need soft skills to motivate and manage others. CEOs and top managers find them very useful for compliance gaining and relationship purposes. These skills also help build trust in workforces as people become empathetic towards each other jobs. Soft skills build win/win situations that lead to organizational success…something that was not realized by leaders in the past.

Social loafers often possess very strong soft skills. They use these skills to manipulate others and get them to do more than their fair share of work. Social loafing can be accomplished without soft skills, but those skills make the job of doing as little as possible much easier.

Transferable skills

Transferable skills are applicable across a wide variety of careers because they are needed regardless of the job or task being performed. These skills include time management, dependability, adaptability, and work ethic.

People in management positions often possess transferable skills, but employees who work mostly independently also use them quite frequently. These skills are necessary for many different situations and, without them, employees often fail to advance within their organizations because they lack basic job requirements such as being on time, working hard, and making sure they complete tasks in a timely manner.

Social loafers often lack transferable skills. They do not work hard, choosing instead to let others do the things that are difficult, and they do complete tasks in a timely manner because they manipulate others into doing it for them. Not surprisingly, social loafers typically do not climb corporate ladders because advancing is not their main goal. They simply want to do as little as possible to get by and collect a paycheck.

Social loafers often possess the hard and soft skills listed above, but they choose not to use them or they use them in a way that allows them to get out of work rather than do the work themselves. They are conniving individuals who like to hide under management's radar and take credit for their coworkers' accomplishments.

Upbringing

Upbringing refers to the ways in which a person was raised from a child to an adult. People have different life experiences as they are growing up, and those experiences often influence their career decisions. For example, a person who grew up on a farm might not want an office job if they had a good experience. However, if they had a bad experience on the farm, then they might try to get an office job rather than work outdoors. Another example is a person who grows up in a regimented household might do well in a military career.

Upbringing could have something to do with people becoming social loafers if they were always getting out of work at home while growing up. It's doubtful that there is any research to support or refute this thinking, but it might make an interesting academic study for an industrial psychologist or sociologist.

Interests

Interests are very influential in career choices because it is natural for people to want to work in with something that they enjoy or like doing. For example, a person who enjoys working outdoors might be a good forest ranger. Along the same lines, a person who enjoys looking for clues in scavenger hunts might be a good detective and an individual who likes to draw might be a good graphic designer.

Social loafers might have a wide variety of interests, but, unfortunately, those interests typically do not pertain to the work they are supposed to be doing. Their main interest at work is making sure they do not have to do anything by having others pick up the slack.

Age

People change as they mature and, understandably, so do their career goals. They might have an idea for a career that seems great when they are young, only to find out that it is not realistic as they get older. An example of this is a boy dreaming of playing major league baseball while in high school who changes his mind in college after playing at a much higher level of competition.

Workplace slackers can choose to social loaf at any age. In fact, they might even get better at it as they age because they are experienced at getting others to comply with their needs. However, their experience matters little if they end up getting called out by management or their coworkers. Hopefully, this is the case in most social loafing situations.

Culture and religion

Race, ethnicity, and religious beliefs influence people's career choices in powerful ways. In fact, these factors have been known to be solely responsible for preventing people from taking certain career paths. An example is a devout Catholic who will not work for an abortion clinic. Other examples include a Muslim who will not work for a dance night club that serves alcohol and a Mormon who refuses to work for a company that distributes pornography.

Some of the more extreme social loafers use culture if it benefits their personal agenda. For example, they might claim that they need to attend church services on a religious holiday even though they do not practice that particular religion. However, it must be noted this action is not the norm because this type of social loafing is now bordering on unethical behavior which is up a rung on the ladder of wrongful workplace activity.

In a nutshell, people choose their careers based on a variety of factors including interests, beliefs, religion, culture, education, skills, and maturity, and observations. They are attracted to a certain field of employment or a specific job and decide that they want to work in that field or do that job so they make a move and begin their career.

Now, let's ask an important question. Keeping all of the above factors in mind, can social loafing actually be a career choice? The answer depends on who you ask, but the author of this book believes the answer is an absolute yes. Employees can choose social loafing as a career by doing only as much as they need to maintain their jobs. Most of their effort is spent figuring out how to personally do as little as possible rather than helping others accomplish organizational goals and objectives.

As a group, social loafers are fairly intelligent people. They know how the politics work within their organizations and play the games necessary to remain in good standing with their bosses. They know what they can get away with before they are "called out" by their coworkers for lack of effort or contribution. In order to stop them from multiplying in workplaces, there must be preventative measures in place...which is why the next section focuses on prevention.

Prevention

Social loafing causes problems in organizations and it is difficult to stop it from completely occurring. However, there are ways to minimize its negative effects, and some of these ways are discussed below.

Establish goals

Goal setting is one method for preventing social loafing because it keeps people focused on the end result. However, these goals have to meet certain requirements before they are established. These requirements assure people are capable of and interested in completing the tasks and achieving the necessary objectives that lead to goal accomplishment. The requirements are listed below.

Understanding

This is the most basic of the requirements because people need to understand what they need to do in order to complete the required tasks and accomplish the necessary objectives. Quite simply, goals that are vague or unclear are geared for failure from the start.

If goals are clear and understandable, then some employees will choose to work towards them rather than avoid working towards them because they do not know what they are supposed to do and are too embarrassed to ask others. Unfortunately, it is not uncommon for people to shy away from doing something that they cannot grasp or do not understand so they end up doing little or nothing and becoming social loafers.

Challenge

Goals that are too simple usually do not maintain the interest of the people working to achieve them. This might seem rather strange since most employees find comfort with tasks they find easy, but it is true because a lack of a challenge creates boredom and a lack of interest. When employees lose interest in the goal, then they also lose interest in doing the work necessary to achieve that goal; thereby becoming social loafers.

Realism

This requirement is much more important than some people realize because it refers to believing that the goal established by management actually can be achieved. Goals that are unachievable cause people to lose the motivation to push forward because they see no point in doing so. They know that their efforts will be futile regardless of the amount of energy they put forth so they choose to become social loafers.

Value

Even if a goal is achievable, it has to have some type of value for employees to believe that the accomplishment is worth their effort. If they see no value, they view their work as pointless and unnecessary. When goals lack value, they turn into little more than "busy work" for the employees working toward them, and it is quite natural for these employees to stop doing that work and turn into social loafers.

Monitor team sizes

Team size is another important concern. Teams that are too large tend to be cumbersome. Members spend a lot of time defining roles, assigning responsibilities, and resolving discrepancies. For instance, a team with 20 members would not work well for the design of a bicycle tire. Member's responsibilities will probably overlap, and social loafing will likely occur.

Another reason to keep teams small is that employees find it more difficult to hide. For example, a four-member team means each member is responsible for 25 percent of the work while members of a ten-member team only have responsibility for about ten percent of the work. A smaller team requires more work from everyone in order to accomplish the objectives set forth for it, and it is more difficult for one member to avoid doing his or her fair share.

An obvious question arises from this team size discussion. What is the correct number of team members? This is a difficult question to answer, but a general rule of thumb is no less than four and no more than ten. This range provides the necessary expertise and is not likely to promote an environment of social loafing.

Establish individual responsibilities

Employees need to know what is expected of them at work, and this applies when they are placed on teams. Expectations should be outlined before the team is assembled so members are not left guessing what they need to do. These responsibilities need to be clearly defined for easy understanding by the team members.

When individual responsibilities are established, the end result is accountability. Accountability helps people feel connected to the overall effort and keeps them motivated to do their part for the team. This prevents social loafing because all team members have designated tasks that are solely their responsibility.

Establish written procedures

This is the easiest method of prevention because any organization can implement written policies. Policies set a clear tone of what is expected of employees working together in teams. They need to know that social loafing will not be tolerated and there will be consequences for this type of behavior.

These policies can be distributed to employees in a variety of ways. They can be handed out, emailed, or posted on employee bulletin boards. However, the best and most effective way to introduce them is during employee training or meetings. Employee signatures indicate they understand the rules involving social loafing, and signatures are difficult to dispute when problems occur. This assures management that discipline can be taken without fear of future legal action.

Monitor team member selection

Avoid hasty decisions when assigning people to teams by taking the time to examine employee backgrounds, skills, and accomplishments. Members need to be selected based on their knowledge and abilities which will help them realize their value and want to contribute.

Also, avoid placing people on teams based on hierarchy status or structural charts. Some of the best teams include members from all levels and aspects of an organization. This allows for creative thinking, better problem solving, and the prevention of social loafing.

Provide feedback on team progress

Management needs to let teams know how they are progressing. Members need to know that they are on the right track with their ideas and solutions, and they should be recognized for their efforts. People like to be acknowledged when they are doing a good job, and this can be done using feedback.

Feedback can also be used to curb social loafing. Employees need to know when they are not contributing enough so they can make the necessary adjustments to improve. Once these weaknesses are brought out into the open, members who are contributing the most can offer encouragement to the loafers to make sure they stay on the right track. The idea is to encourage a solution-oriented group culture rather than a culture of blame.

Require team members to rate each other

Organizations can take a page from education for this prevention method. Employees on teams know which members are working and which members are loafing. Management needs to tap this knowledge in order to properly address social loafing issues. Once the bosses understand the inner workings of the team, they can "call out" those who give the least amount of effort. This stops slacking within the group, and it sends a message that social loafing will not be tolerated.

Promote a teamwork culture

A culture that promotes teamwork will prevent social loafing by encouraging everyone to help each other. However, leadership needs to be directly involved for this to happen. Culture starts at the top of an organization and works its way down into the rank and file. High-level personnel are the only people who have the authority and influence necessary to create a culture that promotes teamwork and prevents social loafing.

Summary

Social loafing that has existed since people have worked together. It occurs in organizations all over the world and creates problems that are often difficult to resolves. It would be difficult, if not impossible, to completely eliminate this phenomenon, but there are ways to reduce its negative impact and keep it from spreading throughout the workplace.

This book explores social loafing as a career choice for workplace slackers. It introduces the subject, discusses its background, exemplifies its occurrences in organizations, highlights the problems it creates, and shows how to minimize its negative influence. Readers gain an understanding of what social loafing is, what it does, and why some employees choose to follow it as a career path.

Congratulations! You now understand more about social loafing in organizations...the career choice of workplace slackers.